El Salvador

Lessons on Love and Resilience

ANNA M. STOUT

Cover art by Fernando Llort.
Cover design and layout by Michelle Starke.

ISBN-10: 0692318313
ISBN-13: 978-0692318317

Cover art by Fernando Llort

"El corazón en el centro representa la fortaleza del pueblo Salvadoreño, con las grecas que lo hacen un corazón Maya como nuestros ancestros, con una rama de olivo en el centro que simboliza la esperanza en los jóvenes que están abajo tomados de la mano como un pueblo que renace en comunidad representado por las casitas. En la parte superior está el maíz, fruto de nuestras tierras con dos pájaros que representan la libertad y la paz."
–Fernando Llort

"The heart in the center represents the strength of the Salvadoran people, with its ornamental patterns that make it a Mayan heart like that of our ancestors. An olive branch in the middle symbolizes the hope vested in the youth, who are holding hands below as a people that is reborn in community, represented by the little houses. At the top is maize, the fruit of our lands, with two birds that represent freedom and peace."
–Fernando Llort

DEDICATION

To Serendipity, my unfailing friend. Your constant company has led me to uncountable fortuitous encounters and experiences. My life is a beautiful product of your presence.

Para todos los becados. Su perseverancia, dedicación, y amor me han alentado todos los días a que siga adelante y a que crea en un mejor futuro para este planeta. Ustedes son la esperanza de su país.

Para El Espino. Mi familia, mi inspiración, y mi otro hogar.

To Dave. My mentor, my friend, without whom there would be none of this.

To Chuck. You encouraged me to fly, both literally and figuratively.

To Michael. You were the first one to listen to and fall in love with El Espino through these tales, and the first one to believe in this project. This book would not have been possible without your unwavering support and encouragement. My adoration is unerring.

To all the people who have believed in the work of the Foundation for Cultural Exchange. You have kept our collective heart beating through this first decade.

CONTENTS

ACKNOWLEDGMENTS

Tremendous gratitude is in order for the many people who provided guidance and feedback throughout this writing process.

A fortuitous encounter in a café one afternoon in the thick of a period of writer's block and doubt brought Phyllis and Jerry Moorman into my life to ease my fears, edit the manuscript, and guide me painlessly through the publishing process.

Rubén Buitrago, Steve Stout, Michael Santo, Torrey Beil, and Armando Arias generously and lovingly served as scrupulous editors, helping to polish the many rough edges of the first manuscript.

I am very honored to have the work of Fernando Llort, El Salvador's most iconic contemporary artist, grace the cover of this book. His art is an unmistakable thread in the vibrant fabric of Salvadoran culture. His willingness to contribute to this project is a reflection of the selfless love he has for his people, *el pueblo salvadoreño*.

Thank you all. This wouldn't have been worthy of print without you.

Some names, details, and orders of events have been changed to protect the privacy of the individuals involved.

While I wish I could include photographs of the many faces that are the inspiration for these stories, they have been omitted for the same purpose.

PROLOGUE

Ten years ago and in the thick of my teenage naïveté, I found myself in El Salvador. I was nineteen and, to my mother's unforgiving chagrin, had just given up the President's scholarship at a reputable university where I had barely completed the first semester of an environmental engineering program. I was poor at physics, which made engineering pretty miserable. I was weary of being what everyone expected of me and was feeling the uneasy tug that comes with that feeling. I wasn't sure what was pulling me, but I knew engineering school wasn't it.

In 6th grade, we watched CNN for Kids every afternoon. The daily reports from exotic, conflicted parts of the world captivated me. I longed to be an international correspondent. The daughter of a journalist, I think it always ran latent through my veins. But as I progressed through school and showed aptitude for math and science, the adults in my life nudged me—sometimes gently, sometimes forcefully—toward an engineering degree. I gradually suppressed my thirst for travel and journalism and followed the path others were paving for me.

I returned to my home town quietly after just one semester. Temporarily, I told myself, trying to shake the stigma of coming back home. After enrolling in the local college for what was to be only one semester (just long enough to "figure things out"), I came across a poster for a summer sociology trip to El Salvador.

That poster reignited something in me. I must sheepishly admit that I did absolutely no research about the country or the culture, and that my justification to my mother for taking the trip (that this was an opportunity to practice Spanish in an immersion format) was an assumption based strictly on the country's name. And had you asked me what sociology was, I would have stood, stammering and staking out an exit.

Nonetheless, I knew I had to go. My mother ushered me to the first trip meeting, knowing that anything that got me out of Grand Junction for a time would be good for me. And a short couple of weeks later, I stepped off the airplane into a land of lush vegetation and stifling humidity that was teeming with life. This was not the dusty tumbleweed setting from the old westerns my dad watched when I was a kid that I was anticipating. I learned my first of many lessons in that moment: El Salvador is not Mexico.

The next 16 days would mark the beginning of my awakening to a world beyond what had been my sheltered reality. I'll spare the lengthy narrative here, but suffice it to say that my ignorance (political, historical, economic, cultural, ad nauseam) was painfully shattered.

But had the impact of the first trip stopped there, this may well have been a very different and, perhaps, bitter book. Instead, what I discovered was that I had a void I had never acknowledged—and suddenly it was full. The love I was offered by the people I met during that first trip, their example of resilience, faith, and perseverance, and their unconditional inclusion of me into their families, rushed into that void until it overflowed.

I begrudgingly returned to the States, primarily because Dave Harmon, the Mesa State College professor who was the engine behind the trip and would soon become my mentor, said to me on the last day with his characteristic grin, "If I return home without you, I'm in big trouble, you know." But I knew I could not let this community simply settle in among my memories; it had to stay alive.

What that first trip set in motion for me and for seven fellow students would soon become the Foundation for Cultural Exchange (FCE), a nonprofit organization we founded in late 2004. Working with the Centro de Intercambio y Solidaridad in El Salvador, the Foundation established Grand Junction's Sister City relationship with El Espino in 2005. Sister Parish, Sister Schools, and Sister Library relationships between the two communities followed.

In 2009, at the community's request, we began a scholarship program for high school and college students in El Espino and surrounding communities. That scholarship program has since become our cornerstone. More than 50 American travelers (we call them delegates) have traveled with the FCE to El Salvador to experience the life and culture of our Sister

City and to *convivir*[1] with the scholarship students and community members. We've raised money for emergency relief, a new building for kindergarten classes, an outdoor auditorium for the school, and more. We've delivered hundreds of pounds of classroom supplies, toys, and books to the community.

November 2014 marks 10 years since this relationship began and this book is a celebration of that first decade. It is a tribute to the people whom I have met and the lessons they have taught me. There are ten chapters that symbolize the ten years we have been working together, written to convey the beauty of the culture as much as the suffering of its people, but especially to pay homage to the resilience, generosity, and warmth of the Salvadoran people. I hope this book tells a story that is distinct from the hopelessness and bloodshed reported in the media, and instead humanizes the struggle for *superación*[2] in El Salvador. Above all, I

---

[1] *Convivir* is one of my favorite words in Spanish, along with *superación*. *Convivir* translates at the most basic level as "to live together with" and can also be rendered as "to spend time with," "to get along with," or "to coexist." But the concept encompasses so much more than that. Rather, it is the act of spending time fraternally with someone, sharing with one another, and enjoying time spent together. It can happen in an afternoon or throughout a lifetime, but is an active and deliberate exchange of experiences.

[2] *Superación* is another word that doesn't translate well into English. Its most common renditions are "overcoming" and "improvement," especially self-improvement. But to *superarse* is much more than to simply overcome or to improve; it is to survive and thrive in the face of daunting obstacles or difficulty. The stories told herein could not be told without this concept, as it is one of the most defining characteristics of the Salvadorans with whom we have worked.

hope it honors the community and people who have shaped my life and enriched me beyond measure.

INTRODUCTION

From up high, El Salvador is a paradise. Endless stretches of verdant hills that look like broccoli and parsley from afar canvas the countryside, flecked with clusters of silver rooftops and stamped with waffled plots of corn and sugarcane fields. Clotheslines strung from trees bow under the weight of the brightly-colored blankets and clothes that dry in the penetrating sun, which dances off the metal homes tucked between the trees. Fuchsia bougainvillea vines climb walls and posts, and crimson-flowered hibiscus trees hang over roadways. It takes an exercise in imagination to look beneath the ceiling of tropical trees and glimpse the struggle and the violence that brew below.

From 1980 to 1992, El Salvador suffered through a civil war that claimed the lives of more than 75,000 people and led to the disappearance of an uncountable number more. The war was the culmination of centuries of oppression by the wealthy elite and exploitation of the poor majority.

The Salvadoran civil war ended just over twenty years ago. It happened *in this lifetime*. And the scars on the daily conscience of its citizens are still raw.

Every Salvadoran past their mid-twenties has horror stories to tell about the war. Stories of how fathers, mothers, children, cousins, and neighbors were slaughtered. How every morning, bodies or parts of bodies would turn up in gutters along the streets. Atrocities most Americans have only seen on screen were a daily reality for the Salvadoran people, and the trauma caused by those experiences remains ever present.

In 1992, twelve years after the official start of the war, UN-brokered peace accords were signed. The end of the war did not bring an end to suffering, though. Despite a formal cease-fire, the root causes of the war were still prevalent: extreme inequality, oppression, poverty, and a dismal lack of opportunity.

Broken families, unemployment, and young people with stunted educations, limited job skills, and little economic opportunity were the war's indelible legacies. The gang violence that eventually rushed in to fill the voids left by war now claims an average of 10 lives every day. El Salvador has the highest homicide rate of children and adolescents and one of the highest overall homicide rates in the world. Its people have become in many ways desensitized to violence because it has been prevalent for decades—and for El Salvador's young people, this means it is the only reality they have ever known.

But there is a resilience so characteristic of the Salvadoran people. Uncertainty is a way of life. Danger is as much a part of the daily routine as getting tortillas for dinner. Yet inside the walls of each house, the trepidation that permeates daily life does not enter. Instead, unwavering faith and the love and support of family fill homes, from which they derive comfort, determination, and purpose.

In a country ravaged by a war that pitted neighbor against neighbor, in communities in which tattooed young men and women reign with fear and command obedience, in a place where—when war and gangs mercifully avert their attention from you—Mother Nature is always perched to destroy your home and habitat with rains, floods, and earthquakes, in *this* place, people are sincerely kind, generous, and loving. Despite poverty, vulnerability, and the peril that stands poised and ready to strike every day, the Salvadoran people are faithful, spiritual, and giving. They are survivors. They are warriors. They are resilient.

The chapters that follow are glimpses into the lives of these people and the challenges they face with determination every day. Each chapter tells the story of survival, of hope, of perseverance, and of what El Salvador is to me.

AHORITA

"If lunch is still walking around the front yard when you arrive, you're not late."

One of the most difficult things to come to terms with when working in a culture so significantly different than one's own is how people view time. I embarked on my first trip to El Salvador as a hopelessly naïve nineteen-year-old, aware there were other worlds out there, but grossly unaware that the life that was so familiar to me could be so foreign to others. Perhaps the hardest element to understand was the Salvadoran orientation to time.

As a child and teenager at my mother's mercy to get from one place to another, I was taught that when calculating the time to leave for an event, you always added twenty minutes to the time it took to get somewhere. We were never late to anything, and in fact were usually the first ones there. I never questioned it. A 2:00 p.m. doctor's appointment began for us in the waiting room at promptly 1:40 p.m.

My early teenage years spent in the Civil Air Patrol further reinforced that. To this day, Captain Ferrin's chastising words ring clearly in my ears: "If you're early, you're on time. If you're on time, you're late. If you're late, it's unacceptable." And as long as I was being toted around by my mom or my beloved surrogate grandpa, I was always early.

My driver's license changed that. Much to my punctual twin sister's daily dismay, I was usually speeding to get to wherever I was going and was lucky to be there two minutes past the start time. Until she bought her own car, which was the better part of our sophomore year, the poor girl was docked constantly for being tardy to first period. My late teens earned me the culturally frowned-upon reputation of living last-minute-to-last-minute and I regularly suffered the consequences of walking in late.

The result was not that I became more punctual, by any stretch. Quite the contrary; I was incorrigible. Nonetheless, the dread each approaching minute to an on-time departure brought would bind my stomach into knots and set my heart racing. I would fight myself and drag my feet, always leaving just past what would have been "right on time."

* * *

Had I done any modicum of research on the Salvadoran culture before I embarked on my first trip outside the country, I would have known that the loose Salvadoran concept of time is drastically different than the staunch American expectation of punctuality. I sheepishly admit I didn't so much as look at a map to prepare for my trip, let alone do any cultural research; my primary goal was to practice Spanish and I assumed by the country's name that I was going to a Spanish-speaking country.

Early into one of my first trips to the country alone, I was invited to a lunch that was scheduled to start at 1:00 p.m. I was to be the guest of honor, and I took my role very seriously. My host family had a series of errands to run in the morning, for which I had gotten up early (which was not a difficult task, given the screeching roosters outside my window that arose long before the sun made its daily debut) and readied myself so as to not slow anyone down. I came out to the kitchen area and sat down, purse slung over my shoulder as if to say, "Ready to leave at a moment's notice!"

An hour passed and the family still bustled about the house finishing early morning chores, seemingly unaware the clock was even ticking. The knot in my stomach took root and I could feel my breathing become shallow as I tried to allay the stress that was creeping over me. As a guest in a foreign land, there was nothing I could do except to try to appear gracious to my host family, which meant being unobtrusive and congenial. But I was mortified at the prospect of arriving late and appearing ungracious to the lunch host. My frustration toward the family's apparent indifference to the lunch invitation was suffocating.

At one point, the youngest son poked his head in the kitchen and said, "*Ahorita vamos,*" and then disappeared. My elementary Spanish understood, "We're leaving *right now,*" so I gathered my things and walked out to the car.

I realized after standing there awkwardly for some time that there had been a misunderstanding. A cultural mistranslation, I would soon discover. I returned to my post at the kitchen table.

The son finally grabbed the keys, close to 11:00 a.m., and we set off down the jagged dirt road toward the San Martin market, some twenty minutes up the Pan-American Highway. I learned to my dismay that we had been requested to procure some of the items needed for lunch, which only increased the pressure I felt to arrive early so they would be able to prepare the food on time.

The clock on the dashboard mocked me as it drew nearer to 1:00 p.m. and we drove farther into the congested market streets with no apparent haste. It seemed that every turn inspired a short detour by my host—a dash into the city hall to pick up a document ("This will just take a minute."), a pop-in at a friend's house to check on something ("We're right here, after all.") a quick stop on the street to buy a snack from the roadside vendors ("You *have* to try green mangoes with lime and chili.")—so by the time we made it to the market, walked through the labyrinth of stalls, and purchased what we had been charged with acquiring, it was after 2:00 p.m. And we were still in a completely different town.

By this point, my anxiety was so intense that I had the courage to press my host. "We're going to miss the lunch," I told him, distressed. "*Tranquila, ahorita llegamos,*" was all he would tell me. There was that word again, *ahorita*, and yet it was obvious he was not using it as I understood it. And *tranquila*—calm—was the last thing I had the capacity to feel at that moment.

Twenty minutes later, we turned off the highway onto a plunging dirt road, flanked by bougainvillea and banana trees, and continued another ten minutes down the patchwork of cinderblock homes surrounded by barbed wire and metal fences, small grazing fields, and stretches of tropical foliage. We made our way to the lunch site and I was convinced we would find it vacant, napkins and lunch remnants scattered on the ground, bony stray dogs foraging through the trash bins for scraps.

To my astonishment, we pulled up to a house with a spacious dirt yard bustling with activity. Women stood over giant cauldrons of steaming liquids, stirring their contents and feeding branches into the fires below them. Men were setting up the red and white plastic tables in the open space, while young people brought out stacks of chairs and placed them around the tables. Children played with a hard plastic ball in an improvised game of soccer while the chickens scattered to avoid their feet.

There was no sign of impatience, distress, or hurt feelings. Our arrival was acknowledged with warm greetings and kisses on the cheek. A young woman came to retrieve the bags of goods we had purchased in the market.

I asked if there was anything I could do to help, feeling foolish at the thought of my exasperation earlier. No, everyone told me, *tranquila.*

I sat down and tried to tune in to any one of the many conversations that were flying past me. My Spanish was still rudimentary and I was just getting used to the sing-song rise and fall of the Salvadoran accent. The exchange that caught my ear caught me off guard.

The woman of the house called out to her daughter. *"¡Agarrá los pollos y traéme mi cuchillo!"* I watched, mouth agape, as the girl grabbed a machete and chased the chickens one-by-one and carried them by the feet, flapping and clucking wildly, to her mother.

Half horrified, half stunned, I realized I had just learned my first profound lesson about time in El Salvador: if lunch is still walking around the front yard when you arrive, you're not late.

PERSEVERANCIA

"The fluffy pile of wood shavings that had gathered at his feet evidenced he had been at it for some time already."

I awoke early one morning to a dull and steady *thud-thud-thud* outside my slatted window. I lay there contemplating whether I could stomach the first cold *guacalazo* of water dumped over my head now or if I should wait to get up and trudge out to the bathroom to "shower" until I was *really* sweating. The thuds continued and the cacophony of roosters, dogs, and street vendors began. So I reluctantly gathered myself up and headed outside.

The first sight that greeted me was the slight, hunched-over body of my adoptive father, *Papá*, deftly wielding his machete against a short shaft of wood. The fluffy pile of wood shavings that had gathered at his feet evidenced he had been at it for some time already.

* * *

Papá had celebrated his eightieth birthday two days prior with little fanfare. He is a small man, not quite reaching five feet tall and barely weighing ninety pounds, with weathered skin and mangled fingers. In the early mornings and late at night, his belabored grunts decry the dull ache that is taking root in his bones. But he gets up every morning before the sun and heads to the land behind his house to clear brush, dig trenches, and plant corn, peppers, coffee, and other small crops, or he starts his ancient, lurching, white-and-rust-colored pickup truck and heads into the community to lend a hand with whatever project—a new well, paving a road, clearing a mudslide—that is in the works at the moment.

I learned about community participation from this man. His quiet example as the president of the local community development association in recent years and his stories about organizing the community to raise money to expand the school (which only went through third grade at the time) and campaigning to implement a running water project in the late 1970s were more didactic to me than any development class I took in college.

Papá also taught me selfless generosity. His wife tells about how when the 81 water spickets were installed in houses throughout the community in 1981 after a three-year, hard-fought campaign, his easily could have been the first. But he insisted on being the eighty-first recipient. When asked why he waited, he says he wanted to make sure that everyone was taken care of first.

With what little he has, there is always enough to give something to the neighbor who comes calling, and he has inculcated this mentality in his adolescent granddaughters. When the FCE comes with donations for children or the school, we typically store items at their house before delivery. Their delight as we go through everything is selfless and genuine; "A little boy is going to *love* this!" and "*¡Qué bonito!* This will be perfect for a little girl!" They have never once asked to keep anything, and when something is offered to them, they politely decline, saying, "There are others who need it more."

But more than anything, *Papá* has taught me perseverance. No matter how early I rise, he is already up chopping, planting, repairing, or studying something. I've found him reading books by lamplight on how to use a computer, and the first time I caught him studying his granddaughters' English primers, he looked up with a grin and motioned to his head, "Maybe it's not too late for this old coconut to learn a thing or two."

* * *

On the day of his birthday, he was out in the *terreno*, his small plot of land, clearing brush when I arrived to surprise him with a cake, complete with 80 small candles. I sent the girls to get him while I lit the cake. He arrived, scythe in hand, just in time to blow out—in one breath—the small blaze that was engulfing the cake.

After finishing his piece, he stood, tendered a polite "*Con permiso*[3]," and went back out to work until nightfall.

---

[3] This is perhaps one of my favorite cultural practices in El Salvador and throughout other parts of Central America. The politeness that is built into the language is admirable; one does not enter a home or business, or take a seat or stand up from the table, without uttering "*con permiso*" (with permission), which, of

The next morning, I sat at the breakfast table and watched *Papá*'s silhouette as he diligently sharpened his weathered machete in the back doorway. He fetched an old sledgehammer, looked it over pensively, and then disappeared into the wooded area behind the house. A short while later, he emerged with a large stick. He settled into his plastic chair in the shade overlooking the drive and began to chop, his slight wrist deliberate in its controlled, rhythmic movements.

When I approached him inquisitively some time later, he showed me the sledgehammer and explained that the head had come loose from its handle from years of use. He was fashioning a new one now, an art that required tapering the handle from the grip area, which would be the narrowest part, to the end that would eventually snugly hold the head. He slid the head on to measure his progress and it stopped about a third of the way up the handle.

Before I retired to bed that night, I saw the handle leaning against the wall with the head fitted about halfway up. The machete lay beside it, as if resting after a hard day's work. I examined its weathered handle, its steely blade, and the sheer size of it. It was probably 20 inches long, fierce and formidable.

For *campesinos* in El Salvador, a machete is an extension of a man, as much a daily accessory as his hat or belt and as utilized as his own hands. Rural Salvadorans learn at a very young age to use machetes for a myriad of household and agricultural uses. The machete also doubled as protection and may be a poor Salvadoran's only weapon.

---

course, is always implied to be granted, but affirmed with "*propio*" or "*tuyo/suyo*" (it's yours).

Papá once told me about a *viejito*, a frail old man, in the community who was shuffling home alone one evening. He was ambushed by a gang member who held out a knife and stated he was *"del Dieciocho,"* meaning he was a member of the Barrio 18 gang, and demanded whatever cash the old man carried. The old man, fed up with the violence and disgusted by the brazenness of the young man, drew his machete from his hip. *"Yo soy del 24,"* he pronounced fearlessly, brandishing his 24-inch blade at the boy. The young man, caught off guard, stammered, then turned and fled.

* * *

I stood in the doorway now and watched this man whom I have come to regard as a father in the soft morning light from a distance now for a few moments, marveling at his determination and resourcefulness, before moving on to my bucket shower and the busy day ahead of me. He was still hard at work whittling the handle when I left around noon, having moved a few times with the sun, chasing the shaded areas around the dirt patio.

I returned just after dark and saw the product of his persistence leaning innocuously against the doorframe. My heart filled with admiration and love for this modest, untiring man. He awakens with a drive that keeps his tiny body abundantly full of life and meaning and goes to bed each night with the aches of a grueling, but purposeful, day.

LA PROXIMIDAD DE LA MUERTE

*"Death is all around her, and it always has been. But in
the depth of those eyes is an undeniable strength and the
understanding that life's fragility makes it precious."*

My great-grandmother died when I was a small child.
I'm not sure what ultimately killed her, but whatever it
was, it can be lumped into the larger category of
afflictions we generally refer to as "old age." The next
experience I would have with death would be my
grandpa's stroke, more than a decade later, which took
him at 87 years of age. After that, we had to put down
our childhood dog, Noel, for snipping at a child's face.
Soon thereafter, my little sister's cat got giardia and we
had to put it down. Death was, for me, something that
happened to old people and animals, and almost always
peacefully.

I met the side of death from which I had been
blissfully sheltered in El Salvador—the kind of death
that makes you question the very existence of a God.

23

News reports of dismembered bodies, targeted shootings in broad daylight, people being hacked to death *a machetazos* (by machetes) are daily occurrences given the brutality of the gang situation in the country.

But even beyond the senseless crimes arising from gang rivalries, the proximity of death, especially in poorer, rural areas, is inescapable. Most Salvadorans experience death very close to them, from classmates caught in the crossfire of gang wars to poisoned pets, from babies who succumb to gastrointestinal illnesses to adults who can't afford treatment for preventable diseases.

Yet even with the imminence of death, the Salvadoran people are not resigned; instead, they have a vitality that emanates from the love they give unreservedly and the value they place on their relationships. I learned this most profoundly from a young girl who seemed to suffer blow after blow, but who has never stopped loving or giving. This is her story.

* * *

Kenia comes from a very broken family. Her conception was accidental and her mother abandoned her as a small child, leaving her in the legal care of her aging maternal grandparents.

The maternal affection that Kenia lacks is compensated by an intense love for animals. One of the first things that impressed me about this young lady was her attention to her pets; they slept on the bed with her, hung out in the house, and generally enjoyed treatment uncommon for animals that typically serve security and pest control roles in the rural countryside.

The most beloved of Kenia's pets was Oso, a puppy she rescued from a trash heap. Oso received a weekly bath, slept with Kenia, and was spared the thin bamboo rod her grandfather regularly threatened all of the other household pets with.

One morning, I awoke to Oso's shrieks, thinking (as is my greatest fear when I am down there) that somebody had broken into the house on account of me. I laid there, terrorized, until Oso came stumbling into my room. Foam gathered at the corners of her mouth and her wild eyes looked at me with the supplication of a creature that knows it is dying.

I woke Kenia and she brushed me aside, reassuring me it was just a cough. Oso's uneven gait confirmed something more was wrong, and I insisted. Kenia got up, rubbing sleep from her eyes, and took in with horror the scene unfolding in the bedroom.

Her immediate reaction was resignation. "She's been poisoned," she said softly and began to cry. This was not the first time this had happened to one of her animals, and she recognized the signs of death creeping over the small animal's body.

I immediately dialed my friend Delia who was studying veterinary medicine in the capital. I could tell that my 6:00 a.m. call had awakened her, but she quickly started barking orders and simultaneously got in her car and began the 45 minute drive to El Espino.

"Give her charcoal," she instructed me.

Kenia looked at me helplessly as I conveyed the message. "Burn a tortilla. Mix it with lime and force her to eat it. I'll be there soon with an I.V.," Delia coaxed.

The look in Kenia's eyes turned from resignation to

determination as she realized there might be a chance to save the pup. She deliberately placed a tortilla on the burner of the small gas stove in her grandmother's kitchen. Each time tears began to well up in her eyes, I followed up with a new, albeit meaningless, instruction to keep her occupied.

By the time Kenia had the charred tortilla concoction ready, Oso was nowhere to be found. I sent Keni out to the wooded land behind the house to look for her, praying to any deity that this wretched little puppy not succumb to the cruel reality of Salvadoran dogs. Kenia returned a short time later with Oso cradled in her arms, her head flopping lifelessly to one side.

After accommodating the dog in a shady area, Kenia gently placed the mixture before the dog, and to our surprise and relief, she lifted her head began to lap it up obediently; she seemed to know that what Kenia offered her was her saving grace. The poor creature's tongue hung futilely between her teeth, but the opaque quality of her eyes seemed brighter.

By the time Delia arrived, Oso could hold her head up on her own, though her tongue still languished in her mouth, and her eyes began to look even hopeful. Kenia dutifully followed Delia's orders, helping her to introduce the IV line into the dehydrated veins of the canine.

Oso miraculously survived that day and I returned to Colorado days later with the relief of knowing she had narrowly escaped the ire of a neighbor who was trying to protect his chickens from the meddling creature. (Another neighbor had alerted Kenia that the neighbor was complaining about the dog killing some of the baby chicks.) All that mattered was that Kenia still had her most precious being.

Less than a month later, I received a phone call in Grand Junction. *"Mataron a la Oso,"* was all the barely-audible voice that spoke to me on the other line could say. I coaxed Kenia to tell me what had happened. Oso was following her to school one morning, despite Kenia shooing her away, and a pickup came careening down the road. The truck did not slow as Oso stepped out in front of it. Kenia called the number she had scrawled on her concrete bedroom wall after the poison incident, but Delia informed her there was nothing that could be done; the internal injuries were too severe.

Oso writhed in pain that afternoon and into the evening. Kenia did not eat that night. She held Oso in her lap as the puppy's big brown eyes pleaded for help. Kenia held in her sobs until the puppy's soft whine finally faded.

It would take some time to get over Oso, but Princesa, the scrawny, skittish puppy her boyfriend had brought to the house about a week before, would help ease the transition. By now, Kenia has learned to channel her love from one creature to the next, never taking for granted the time she has with them, but never getting too used to their presence. So far, none has lived long enough to die naturally.

* * *

A year after Oso's passing, with her high school graduation imminent, Kenia busied herself with research for her senior thesis. She was working on the project with three other classmates, one of which was her best friend.

Kenia awoke to her grandmother's gentle voice. *"Keni, te buscan."* One of her schoolmates had come looking for her. The news she delivered buckled Kenia's knees. She dropped to the ground outside the back door and wept. Princesa approached her, head down and tail lowered, tenderly nudging her and licking her tear-strewn face. Finally, she gave up and rolled over in a helpless attempt to comfort her friend.

Keni's best friend and best friend's mother were murdered in their home that morning by gang members who broke in in the early morning hours, drug the family out of bed, and opened fire. The brother and father were gravely wounded, as well.

Kenia had lost classmates before, but never one this close to her. The two of them had been together just days before the murder.

There are two versions of why the family was targeted; one is that the girl was dating a boy from rival gang territory (though it is said she didn't know about his gang affiliation) and that the gang from her neighborhood was sending out a message: respect the gang that controls the territory in which you live. The second version is that somebody in her family had snitched on or otherwise offended a gang member and thus earned the "green light" for their attack. I never got the full story, but the truth hardly matters when whole families are being massacred.

The nightmares began that night, and Kenia's younger sister, Valeria, began sleeping with her the next night. Kenia has not slept without Valeria since, which means Princesa has been relegated to sleeping outside with the rest of the dogs.

The Salvadoran media is saturated with daily stories

of murders and tragedy, principally suffered at the hands of the gangs. Some people are targeted because of their association with gang members, others for simply being in an area controlled by rival gangs of the territory in which they live. And still others are just caught in the crossfire of territory disputes and assertions of strength and control, especially in public transport. Many communities straddle gang lines, which means that a short ride in a bus can prove fatal as it crosses from one territory to another.

As many Salvadorans relate, the choice to leave the house each day can prove to be a matter of life or death. Yet there is no other option; one must go to the market, to work, to school, to visit family. You keep your head down and your valuables ready to hand over, and never leave the house without a blessing.

* * *

A month after her best friend died, Kenia was caring for three kittens that one of the housecats refused to nurse. The five-week-old kittens were half the size they should have been, but they were surviving. After a few weeks of nurturing, the mother had even begun to clean and feed them at Kenia's coaxing.

One night, a stray cat entered the house through a broken window slat. A melee ensued in the main room and by the time the family had turned on the lights and could comprehend what was happening, the mother cat had driven out the stray. The favorite kitten, a malnourished black-and-white runt with a pointy, mouse-like face, was nowhere to be found. The explanation was that the stray cat had carried it off to eat it. We searched the neighborhood the next day for the baby, but found nothing.

A week later, Kenia moved a mattress that had been leaning against the wall. Behind it she found the little black-and-white kitten, its paws and stomach chewed off. She cried harder for the kitten than she had for her friend, as the cumulative pain of so many deaths wrenched her heart.

* * *

When I next saw her, the two kittens were thriving and Princesa was on her heels wherever she went. She had a new creature, a baby squirrel that had fallen from a tree, and was fully enveloped in the love and care of all her animals. There had been a shooting nearby in the days before I arrived and she had gone to see the cadaver before the police carted it off. As she told me about it, I couldn't help but admire the tenderness with which she stroked the squirrel while she described the carnage. "*Pobrecita la gente,*" she said softly. Poor things.

Kenia's black eyes are profound beyond her years. They reflect the pain of her mother's rejection, the nightmares she has about her aging grandfather dying, the images of the dead bodies she has observed at close range from behind police tape, the loss of animals well before their little bodies could age enough to die naturally, and the wise comprehension of what is happening in her country. Death is all around her, and it always has been. But in the depth of those eyes is an undeniable strength and the understanding that life's fragility makes it precious. Kenia loves without reservation.

SUPERACIÓN

"The heightened sense of alarm we all had seemed to dissipate, or at least subside, the second we sat down around the table."

The day was tranquil; I spent it with my fourteen-year-old goddaughter sitting for hours working at our makeshift office on a plastic picnic table tucked beneath a low canopy of trees behind the house. *Papá* busied himself around the house fixing this, cleaning that, and *Mamá* was at the half-finished chapel on the edge of their small plot in prayer with other women from the neighborhood.

She and my *Papá* donated the land to the community a few years prior to build the modest structure in which neighbors could gather to pray and hold religious events. The progress was slow, as it relied on the contributions that trickled in from the community. But even before the roof was completed, when piecemeal plastic tarps still stretched across where the ceiling would soon be, often precariously pregnant with rainwater, I never saw a day pass that my *Mamá* didn't head down to the chapel with her Rosary and prayer book.

From where we sat under the trees, I could hear the soft notes of the women's *alabanzas*, or songs of praise, carrying over the sound of the masons scraping at mortar and cinderblocks. Insects buzzed around my computer screen and the throaty calls of exotic birds rang out above us. The shade of the thick foliage and the gathering cloud cover made the humid afternoon not only bearable, but actually pleasant.

When day finally gave way to evening, I headed inside to get ready to go out for dinner with my soldier friend. Instead I found a text message from him that said, "Um, I recommend we don't go anywhere today. There's a country-wide curfew in effect. Just for today. Two buses were already shot up [with machine guns]." My soldier friend isn't afraid of anything, so this was serious.

A few minutes later, my local cell phone rang. Another admonishment from a friend: "Anna María, don't leave the house tonight. The buses have all stopped running. People are scared. They're calling it Black Friday." It was 6:30 in the evening. It had just gotten dark.

Earlier that day, I was getting ready to walk to a close friend's house for a visit, only to realize that he and his mother and sister were evacuated from the country earlier that week due to threats of extortion and violence from the gangs. My friend was one of the lucky few with the resources and connections available to flee the country quickly—and legally.

I would later find out that after a few months of asylum in the United States, my friend and his family would pay the $4,000 extortion to be able to return to their home. They suspect they know the identity of their extorters, but the risk of going to the authorities is too great; retaliation is bloodier than the threats made in the first place.

These things have become so commonplace in El Salvador that I am almost immune to the alarm they cause. But this night was different. I was unsettled.

What was happening that night was called the *Sombra Negra*, or the Black Shadow. The name is a throwback to paramilitary death squads composed primarily of off-duty police and soldiers that emerged toward the end of the war in 1989. These vigilantes famously target criminals and gang members, citing the government's impotence and unwillingness to enforce laws and combat illicit activity. Their modus operandi is to move by the cover of night, hooded and masked. They go to known gang members' homes (these are officers with access to intelligence), and, claiming to be police or the army, force their way in, then execute the gang members.

The previous Friday, the *Barrio 18* (18 Street) gang imposed a curfew in a community and christened it *Viernes Negro* (Black Friday). Tonight's Black Friday was the *Sombra Negra's* response to that.

With the cautions of my two friends reverberating in my ears, my *hermanita*, or little sister, and I walked her friend home so he wouldn't be on the streets alone. As we walked, we saw a few buses replete with passengers pass by caravan-style, presumably seeking strength in numbers. This was the last run of the night, hours before the buses usually make their final passes.

The interior lights were on in every bus. I could see the people's expressions through the windows—faces drawn, brows furrowed. No one seemed to be talking or looking at each other. Amid the apprehension, weariness permeated the air.

We reached his house, exchanged tense goodbyes, and turned back toward home. The same buses that had just passed were now coming back the opposite direction—empty. They had not continued along their routes, but rather had let their fares off at the edge of safety and were returning a different way.

We walked fighting the urgency to run, placing each foot deliberately on the ground in a futile attempt to conceal the acceleration of our hearts by controlling our footsteps. We kept our heads down with the logic of a child who pulls the covers over his eyes and leaves his head exposed: if I can't see them, they can't see me. I don't think either of us uttered a sound until we crossed the threshold of our concrete home and felt the heavy metal door latch behind us with the comforting, steely echo that reassured us we were safe.

The silence that followed was eerie, except that it was not silent. What was missing was the roar of the trucks and buses that pass in front of the house all night long. But in that void of sound, the pops and explosions in the distance were more prominent and numerous than normal. Every unnerving rat-tat-tat-tat that perforated the stillness, every reverberating boom, every staccatoed flurry sent my mind racing through a litany of violent scenarios. Of course, as I was taught there, it would always come to rest on the comforting, though fallacious, conclusion that somewhere somebody was celebrating something, and that the terror that played through my mind was, in fact, just the jubilance of fireworks.

Dinner that night was one of the strangest juxtapositions of feelings I have ever experienced. The heightened sense of alarm we all had seemed to dissipate, or at least subside, the second we sat down around the table. *Mamá* even joined us. *Papá* grunted when his plate was placed before him and, in his gravelly voice, grumbled that it was too much food. Then he looked up at me, winked through his sturdy, square-rimmed seventies glasses, and with a sly smile said, "I'm trying to lose some weight." I would be surprised if his bony body weighs more than 90 pounds.

After *Papá* mumbled a prayer, we began eating our simple dinner of rice, fried plantains, and refried red beans. The only sounds that broke the silence were whispered requests to pass the tortillas and *Papá* barking, "*¡Fuera, fuera!*" as he whipped a switch on the floor at the dogs that tried to sneak undetected through the gaps in the decorative metal outer door.

Before long, we heard an especially long and measured series of pops, the space between each shot too calculated to be fireworks. I looked at the younger sister and asked her if they were gunshots or fireworks. She shrugged, "You never know," though I think we all knew.

The older of the two girls had recounted to me earlier while we washed up for dinner that a bus driver and his *cobrador*, the man who walks up and down the crowded aisle jingling a grimy cloth coin purse and collecting riders' bus fares, had been killed a few weeks ago down the hill past the house on the same route the buses refused to traverse on this night. She awoke to the sounds of what she chalked up to *cohetes*, fireworks, only to discover the next morning it was the machinegun fire that had taken the men's lives. She walked with her boyfriend to the crime scene early the next morning and saw the bloody bodies from behind a skimpy strip of caution tape.

At that, *Papá* took a sip of his thick corn *atól* and the thick film that had cooled on the top slopped out of his mug down his chin. He spit it on the concrete floor and I looked at him with feigned disapproval. "One of my intestines came out," he replied apologetically. The whole table erupted in a combination of groans and laughter.

A few minutes later, as I rose to clear the empty serving dishes to lure the swarms of flies away from the table, he motioned to me. I stopped in the doorway as he began waving his hands theatrically at the chair opposite him and with a flourish, threw both hands forward. Instantaneously, the chair jumped. Again, we burst into laughter at his childish trick.

Mamá began telling stories of *Papá's travesuras*, his mischievousness, to the delight of the girls and me. She carried us to a time when his bones didn't ache, thick black hair covered his head, his truck started without first saying a prayer and then jiggling a wire, and his sagacious wisdom seemed impossible. By the time dinner was over, the *Sombra Negra* was no more real to us than the boogey man or *el mico*[4].

---

[4] "*El Mico Brujo*," or "The Witch Monkey," is a legend passed down for generations in El Salvador about men and women who could leave their souls in a *guacal* (bowl) at night, take the form of a long-tailed monkey, and head out to cause mischief.

GENEROSIDAD

"Tenga," she told me. *"Se la regalo."*

In June of 2005, the mayor's office of San Pedro Perulapán was gearing up to inaugurate a delivery of heavy machinery that had been donated by some foreign government. San Pedro is the municipality to which El Espino belongs and houses the city hall, mayor's office, civil registry, and other town buildings. The mayor had invited our small delegation to the celebration and we squeezed out of the cramped minivan with trepidation upon seeing the commotion in the plaza.

The town was abuzz. Throngs of people lined the streets and clustered outside of buildings in anticipation of the ribbon-cutting ceremony that would be performed shortly by the mayor and Chinese delegates. I pushed my way up the walkway to the long city hall building painted boastfully in the left-wing's stark white and red party colors, clumsily bumping through the hordes of people, where a lunch alongside the mayor awaited my group.

A young girl, no older than 16 or 17, stood along the path in a simple white tank top with a heart design across the chest. As I passed her, I smiled and complimented her shirt in my heavily-accented and poorly-pronounced Spanish. *"¡Qué bonita blusa!"* She responded with a shy smile, lowered her eyes, and was swallowed up by the crowd.

A short time passed and I sat in the garden patio behind the mayor's office balancing a Styrofoam plate heaped generously with rice, vegetables, chicken, and tortillas on my knees.

As I lifted the thick corn tortilla to my mouth, a petite hand gingerly tapped my shoulder. I turned around to see another hand extended toward me with a small folded bundle in a thin plastic black bag. I raised my eyes to the face of the young lady I had passed earlier, now dressed in a modest black shirt.

"Tenga," she told me. *"Se la regalo."* I sat for a moment, unable to comprehend this simple gesture. But her kind and expectant smile assured me there was nothing to misunderstand. I worked the small knot open and peered in the bag. There, folded neatly, was the white tank top she had been wearing earlier.

The lump in my throat obstructed the clumsy Spanish that was scrambling to form on my lips, so instead I stood to hug her. This young lady had literally just given me the shirt off her back. Her returned embrace acknowledged gently that she understood my unspoken message, and with that, she smiled sweetly, turned, and disappeared around the corner of the building, enveloped once again by the swarm.

I sat, astounded, and held the small shirt in my hands. All of the commotion that swirled around me faded for a moment as I contemplated the beautifully coincidental design, knowing this simple emblazoned heart would forever have an impact on my own.

LA CRUEL NATURALEZA

"In the 15 or 16 trips I had made to the country at that point, I had experienced heavy rain, no doubt, but nothing that had ever been so crippling to the country."

In October of 2011, El Salvador experienced a weather phenomenon that left the country in shambles. Tropical Depression 12-E hit Central America and soon became a strong monsoon, relentlessly dumping almost 16 inches of rain (roughly the equivalent of the country's average yearly rainfall) over the course of 10 consecutive days, breaking a record set in 1969. The storm was the worst natural disaster the country had seen in more than a decade, since the back-to-back earthquakes in 2001.

I arrived late on Saturday and the rains began on Monday night. Initially, the rain was just a nuisance. My friends and I tried to go watch a national soccer game in the capital on Tuesday evening. The rain was coming down so hard that the windshield wipers were useless;

we stayed on the roadways by following the blurry taillights of the cars in front of us. The game was delayed almost two hours as we sat drenched in the stands in the pointless plastic ponchos we bought outside the stadium. When the rain finally let up enough to blow the first whistle, the pools on the field were so deep that the ball did not roll or bounce, but rather would splash to a halt and then sit, floating feebly on the field.

My itinerary that trip included a two-hour excursion (in good weather and good traffic) to a town called Juayúa, about 90 kilometers from San Salvador, where I had a relationship with an artisan from whom I regularly bought paintings and other art pieces. This trip was crucial because we needed gifts for a fundraiser scheduled at the end of October.

El Salvador's terrain is mountainous—the country is known as the Land of Volcanos—and the undulating roadways are hacked through hillsides, leaving towering dirt walls that line the streets with menacing height, poised to come sliding down with the right amount of heavy rain. This was the right amount.

I counted 10 mudslides on the road to Juayúa alone, and another seven on the short drive from Juayúa to neighboring Concepción de Ataco (barely 10 kilometers). Some blocked the whole roadway and we had to drive off the road to get around them, others had knocked cars clean off the road, and still others had carried with them massive trees and power line poles. Whole sections of the road were under water, which made both staying within the lines and avoiding the gigantic potholes nearly impossible.

When we arrived in Juayúa, every shop was shuttered, including the one I came all this way for, and there wasn't a soul in the streets. The trip had taken more than three hours and it was all for nothing.

As we made our way back to the capital, I grumbled the whole way, completely inconvenienced by the situation. "This country has experienced rain for centuries. How has it not figured out how to deal with it by now? How can whole towns be closed because of a rainstorm?"

The next day I made my way to El Espino with a blindly optimistic list of things to accomplish before heading home on Friday. Mother Nature would see to it that nothing would be crossed off that list.

I would spend four days in El Espino without leaving the house. It was too muddy to drive the dirt roads in the community and what with the constant risk of mudslides along the sides of the roads, it was too risky anyway. The Ministry of Education canceled classes nationwide (and having seen our little school become a small body of water with just a typical afternoon's rain, I understood why) so I wasn't able to deliver the donation of books to the school that I had lugged down in two suitcases or visit with the scholarship students.

In the 15 or 16 trips I had made to the country at that point, I had experienced heavy rain, no doubt, but nothing that had ever been so crippling to the country. It took almost five days before I realized the real gravity of the situation.

I woke up on my second morning in El Espino to the morning newscast. The family was gathered around the small television. My entrance was barely noticed as I quietly settled into the hammock strung from the rebar rafters. The whole program was dedicated to call-in updates on road closures, mudslides, crop losses, flooding, homes being washed away, and even deaths. The images that played across the screen were astounding, and it hit me that they were taking place *right outside our door.*

The only sounds that were audible above the television were the occasional sucking of air, followed by heavy sighs and the quietly muttered, "*Pobrecita la gente.*" The channel reported a bridge had collapsed on the border with Honduras and cross-border trade had been all but halted.

I would later learn that eight bridges collapsed and another 37 were damaged. Twenty-one rivers burst their banks. Ten percent of the country (almost 2,000 square kilometers) ended up under water, and at least 60 percent of the country's crops suffered damage. The inconvenience I had felt days before felt downright shameful now.

On my third idle day in the community, one of our oldest scholarship students texted me: "It's really nasty here in El Limón [a neighboring community to El Espino]. The streets are filled with water and here by my house there is an area where there are sometimes mudslides. I want to see you, too, mom, but the way it's raining, I can't go out." He followed that up with a recommendation to curl up with some coffee and sweet bread and take a nap under a warm blanket. I'm not exactly the nap-under-a-warm-blanket type, but I was left with few options.

I had never felt so impotent in my life. The family prohibited me from leaving the home. Electricity was spotty, so I didn't dare run down my laptop battery. In any case, Wi-Fi had gone down on the first day and would not come back by the time I left, so there wasn't much point anyway. (I was staying in the home of one of the comparatively wealthy families in the community, but money couldn't even keep the Wi-Fi on in the face of this crisis.)

The head of the household, a successful, hardworking egg farmer, seemed equally as uncomfortable with idleness, but he handled it much more gracefully than I did, tending to small tasks around the house and napping intermittently in the hammock. I sat for hours one day talking with this normally reserved, taciturn man about everything within mental reach in an effort to avoid going stir-crazy.

Taking his lead, and since I couldn't venture outside, I resigned myself to a strange form of solidarity with the rest of the country. I stopped fighting the weather (as I had on Tuesday and Wednesday while I selfishly griped that the whole country had shut down and *I* couldn't get anything worthwhile done) and instead stayed inside spending time with the family, waiting idly for the downpour to subside and reverently observing the incredible power of the storm from behind the wrought-iron bars of my bedroom window.

I realized in those long, soggy days why family ranks so high on the hierarchy of values in this country. In moments like those you are stuck with them and they are all you have. Furthermore, reading and hearing about death that is occurring simultaneously, you have no idea if what's happening outside might turn to tragedy for you or one of your loved ones.

And conversely, I suddenly understood why time and deadlines are so ephemeral here; so much of what happens that dictates your schedule is beyond your control.

My egotistical frustrations early on made me reflect guiltily on the implications this kind of weather phenomena has on development. After (im)patiently "riding out the storm," I walked away with a profound, firsthand understanding of the challenges developing countries like El Salvador face. El Salvador's infrastructure is still in its infancy when compared with areas of the United States or other developed countries that regularly experience heavy rains.

Everything here just comes to a halt—roads flood, mudslides cut off transportation routes, stores close, school is suspended, people stay home. Or people are evacuated from their homes. This seems to happen relatively often (in this case there were more than 56,000 evacuees) and the government simply cannot keep up.

Retaining walls along roads are not reinforced (if they are built at all), drainage systems are extremely inadequate, houses are built in washes and ravines, and the list goes on far beyond my elementary understanding of architecture and engineering. Even if the country were to overcome the challenge of only having half the year to be able to carry out projects, the government lacks the funds and resources to do so.

Simply put, El Salvador might take a couple steps forward in terms of development, but a few days of heavy, incessant rains are enough to knock it backwards by miles. This is an incredible challenge for a country that is making genuine efforts to advance and join the developed world on the global stage, and poses immense threats not only to such lofty goals as sustainable development, but more immediately, to basic survival itself.

* * *

As my flight took off on Saturday morning, I clutched the armrest in anticipation of the turbulence that lay ahead. But once we broke through the clouds, I looked down and took in one of the most peaceful vistas I had ever seen: perfectly white, fluffy clouds stretched out flat on every side as far as the eye could see. I couldn't believe something so placid and picturesque was wreaking so much havoc on my tiny country below.

UNA LECCIÓN EN ASISTENCIA

"Despite the tragedy we had born witness to, tremendous
satisfaction filled the hearts of the delegates."

Hurricane Ida made landfall in Central America in early November of 2009. Immediately after it passed, a low pressure system arrived, bringing with it more heavy rains. From November 6 to November 9, El Salvador was pummeled with rains that caused flooding, landslides, damage to infrastructure and crops, the evacuation or displacement of thousands of residents, and almost 200 deaths.

After the rains subsided and the damage was assessed, we learned that El Espino was largely spared. But so many of its residents still live in mud brick homes or under plastic tarps intended serve as temporary shelters. The tarps had been distributed by the international relief community after the devastating earthquakes of January and February 2001 and, eight years later, were still primary living quarters for many families across the country.

Three such homes had been completely destroyed in one of the more impoverished sectors of the community. The FCE and the Grand Junction-based Sister Parish, Immaculate Heart of Mary Catholic Parish, conducted an emergency funding drive to raise enough money to help those families rebuild their homes, this time with corrugated metal, cinderblocks, and materials that would be more resistant to rain and earthquakes. We sent down more than $3,000 in December and the homes were inaugurated in May of 2010.

When I arrived in August of 2010 with a delegation in tow, the community suggested adding a visit to those homes to the group's itinerary. Four of the delegates were parishioners at the Sister Parish and had been involved in the fundraising efforts. And so we arrived in the back of a pickup truck one afternoon and eight or nine grade school-age kids greeted us with curious eyes as we clambered down from the rickety vehicle.

The first home was situated on the edge of a small cluster of houses that all shared a common cooking area, large open dirt area (without a doubt, most often used as the children's soccer field), and an outhouse off to one side. These compounds are common among extended families in rural areas in Latin America because they allow for burden-sharing with meal preparation, childcare, and living costs.

One of the older boys led us around to a house that was almost blinding in the sun that shone off its metal walls. The home had not borne the brunt of a whole rainy season and the elements had yet to oxidize the aluminum walls. A table draped with a white tablecloth and flanked by blue plastic lawn chairs was arranged just outside the front door beneath an awning. Metal homes swelter in the Salvadoran heat, so most of one's time at home is spent outside in the shade while the house serves a primary function of providing storage and sleep areas.

Just behind the compound and down a couple makeshift steps made of broken chunks of flat concrete was the second house. The woman of the house was the only one home, but she shyly ushered us in to see inside. We stepped into a surprisingly spacious structure that had a concrete floor, sturdy two-by-four frames, and the same aluminum walls as the first house. The space was divided by a pink shower curtain with small bunches of flowers that hung from the exposed A-frame that sustained the roof, effectively creating both a kitchen area and a bedroom. In the bedroom, sparsely furnished with a large wooden armoire, a plastic chair, and a sagging mattress, they had affixed large pieces of thin, used plywood to the walls to buffer the heat. The faded upside-down graffiti tag "13" (a symbol of the country's most powerful gang, the Mara Salvatrucha) scrawled in spray paint on one of the pieces of repurposed plywood was an ironic contrast to the children's artwork and religious calendar that adorned the walls and the notebooks and school uniforms strewn about the room.

The first boy's mother, father, and little sister joined us at the second house and both families told of the horror they experienced in the few long days of rain and winds that Ida brought with her. They described how even before the hurricane, rain would blow in through the gaps between the ceiling and walls and leak through the holes in the plastic and how everything they owned would get wet. When it would rain (and it rains constantly from March through September) the family would pile things in the center of the room, put plastic sheets over larger objects, and huddle away from the walls until it stopped.

Ida's gale-force winds, on the other hand, brought the rain in almost horizontal sheets that shredded through the plastic tarp in which one of the families lived (their mud home had been destroyed in the earthquakes) and toppled the bamboo poles to which it was attached. The mud home in which the other family lived turned to sludge with the besieging of the rains and collapsed, trapping and almost killing their youngest son. Both families fled to the homes of relatives nearby and had been living in cramped quarters for months until the new structures were completed.

Before we left, the woman of the second home proudly posed next to her small olive-colored refrigerator and electric four-burner stove, luxuries that were unthinkable in her old home because it was too dangerous to run electricity to a place that regularly got so wet.

The third and final home was at the bottom of a gully just across the dirt road from the first two. Its only access route was a treacherous descent about 50 steps down. Each earthen step was about a foot-and-a-half wide by four feet long with a bamboo log at the front that held the dirt in place and partially overgrown with the dark green vegetation so characteristic of El Salvador. It was August and it had rained the night before, so each step was soggy and potentially slippery. We all cautiously made our way down, some stopping to catch their breath about halfway there.

At the bottom, we met the 94-year-old woman who was living in the newly-built metal home. She was blinded decades before in a cooking accident and had lived ever since in a small house next to that of her son and his wife.

Her daughter-in-law recounted the devastating day that the countryside that rises up around them became so impregnated with rainwater that it could not stick to the hills any longer. The mud spilled down the slopes with the force of a moving train and carried with it trees, rocks, and fences. It slammed into her home, demolishing the weak adobe structure. As the walls crumbled on top of her, she fell backwards and felt something slam into her stomach, knowing immediately she had lost the twin boys she carried inside of her and almost certain she would also die under the rubble.

The new home was little recompense for the tragedy the family had lived through, but they told us that it brought them peace of mind, knowing it was sturdier than the old one had been and that it would be able to withstand future storms.

As we climbed back up the almost vertical steps, the group didn't say much. The quiet hope that accompanies stories of survival and the awe at how comparatively little it takes to make a large difference in communities like El Espino were all that was palpable as we climbed back into the pickup and headed to the host homes. Despite the tragedy we had born witness to, tremendous satisfaction filled the hearts of the delegates, knowing they had played a part in these survival stories.

* * *

In November of 2011, as I hand-delivered three suitcases of gifts and school supplies that had been collected by a family in Grand Junction for the most disadvantaged children in El Espino, I found myself at the homes that had been constructed with FCE funding after Hurricane Ida. As we pulled up in the lurching pickup truck we had coined "Santa's sleigh" for those days of deliveries, my heart sank.

The first home that had stood so brilliantly in the sun was shuttered. There were no signs of the table and chairs. I inquired of the children where the family was. "*Los papás se fueron al Norte y los niños se están quedando con la abuela,*" responded one of the boys. The parents, apparently unable to make ends meet on the father's meager wage as a security guard, had immigrated to the United States, leaving their three children in the care of a grandparent. I asked if the home was still used for anything and one of the boys ran to grab a key to let me inside. He returned jingling a key ring and, after unsuccessfully trying each of the keys, shrugged and ran off to deposit the keys where he had found them.

What awaited me at the bottom of the gulley was even more dismaying. As I stepped off the last step and emerged through the thick vegetation into the small clearing, I saw sticks where the old woman's house once stood. No one was home, so I asked the train of children who had come in tow what had happened to the house. The answer was simple: the metal was needed elsewhere, so the house was slowly dismantled. The only house that still stood and served its purpose was the second one with the olive refrigerator.

I was contemplative on the way home. I was grateful for the noise of the pickup, the wind whipping my hair against my face, and the bone-jarring ride on the rough dirt roads because it gave me the distance I needed to process what had happened. More than disheartened, I felt foolish. The quick-fix nature of what we had done felt so satisfying when we visited the homes the year before, but the root of the problem prevailed—crippling poverty that drives people reluctantly away from their homes and families, prevents people from being able to protect themselves from a ruthless and unforgiving environment, and necessitates dramatic decisions for basic survival.

I understood that if we really are to contribute to the development and advancement of this—or any—community, we must address the root causes. And this means empowering people to help themselves and to identify and find solutions to those problems.

MÁS ALLÁ DE MAÑANA

"It's not that I don't want her to study. It's just so hard.
I'm all alone."

"I'm not continuing in the program next year," she
said, lowering her eyes and clasping her hands in her lap.

"*¿Cómo?*" I stammered, feeling my face tingle, as if
my sinking heart were pulling all the blood from it. My
stomach knotted up and my shoulders folded forward,
collapsing in on the void left by my lungs that suddenly
couldn't inflate. "Why, *hija?* What happened?"

"My *mami* says I need to go out and find work to
help her. She said I can work and go to college next year
or the year after." Her voice quivered as she tried to
sound matter-of-fact. Her eyes met my gaze and she
shrugged feebly.

This was the day of her high school graduation, a day
that two years ago was completely out of reach before
she was granted this scholarship. We had just come
from the ceremony at the school and now were

57

gathering with all of the scholarship students and their families to celebrate the achievement of the four graduating scholarship students.

We had not been there two minutes before Jimena (hee-men-uh) tugged at my arm and pulled me around to the back of the house to deliver the news. "I didn't want to spoil the ceremony for you," she explained ruefully. "But her mind is made up."

We spoke for a few more minutes, me pleading with her, her respectfully dodging each of my supplications. At one point her eyes brimmed, precisely when I asked her what *she* wanted. "*No importa.* I have to help my mom with the house." But her eyes belied her; it *did* matter.

Two little kids came tearing around the corner, shrieking gleefully in a game of *mica*, or tag. They froze when the saw us and the tears we both tried to wipe away. Sheepishly, they retreated back where they had come from and the screams ensued.

I looked at Jimena, squeezed her hand reassuringly and told her we would go talk to her mother tomorrow, and to enjoy the graduation *fiesta* because it wouldn't be her last.

* * *

The next day, I asked my *Papá* to accompany me to Jimena's. I called our *promotora*, the woman who oversees the scholarship program and other projects and activities carried out by the FCE in the community. We picked her up in my dad's rickety miracle of a pickup truck and made our way to the single-room mud home where Jimena and her mother, older brother, older sister, and nephew lived.

Jimena was the youngest of the bunch. Her sister had gotten pregnant and dropped out of school to care for the baby and her brother worked full and arduous days while he attended the university part-time. Her mother, a single mother since the children were very little, was illiterate and made $2-3 dollars per day helping a neighbor make and sell tortillas. (Tortillas sell for about $0.12 apiece, so it's hardly a lucrative endeavor for anyone in the rural countryside.) She had recently fallen and suffered a back injury so she couldn't be on her feet for long hours *torteando* anymore, so the family was living on her brother's meager income and the small scholarship stipend Jimena drew each month.[5]

When we arrived, her 23-year-old brother was waiting for us at the top of the path that leads down to the house. We picked our way down the uneven makeshift steps made of broken pieces of concrete, large rocks, and a section of old tires.

A man I had never seen before was leaning in the doorway when we turned the corner to the house. He introduced himself as Jimena's maternal uncle, and I would later learn that Jimena had called him the night before and he had traveled by bus from two hours away to be present for the meeting with her mother.

---

[5] The scholarships granted by the FCE do not have strict rules for how they are spent, as long as the student's education-related expenses are covered. The small stipend is disbursed monthly so that it cannot be misappropriated on large non-educational expenses and so it stretches for the length of the school year. Nonetheless, it is meant to supplement the family's income so the family can afford to send their child to school rather than having the child work to help contribute to the family income.

"*Con permiso*," I said as I stepped over the mound of dirt that runs at the base of the doorframe to keep rainwater from coming in. Her mother received us just past the threshold and greeted us with the traditional kiss on the right cheek. Her dark eyes, set deep in her face, were weary. The lines around her eyes and mouth were testament to her years of struggle and exertion.

We sat down around the streak of morning light that jutted in through the doorway, overlooking the dipping hills to the east that cradle El Espino's nine *sectores*, or neighborhoods. The home, made of mud and adobe, was windowless. Her mother sat to my left at the top of the beam of sunlight, her reticent gaze perpendicular to my seat's orientation and fixated on something outside ahead of her. Jimena angled her chair toward us directly to my right, though not in a triangular shape.

I remember thinking how awkward the setup was, compounding the already uncomfortable situation. The *promotora* sat a few feet away, closer to the doorway, off to one side. My *Papá* situated a chair just outside the door where he could take in what was said without making his presence imposing, and the uncle leaned against a four-by-four that held up the overhang of metal roof in front of the door. Jimena's brother floated somewhere behind me in the penumbra of the house, to which my eyes were still adjusting.

Her mother's expression was indecipherable, obscured in part by shadows, and concealed in part behind the proud lines of her face. Her blue-black hair was streaked with gray strands that sprouted at her temples, fixed at the base of her neck in a smart bun. Wisps of it had come loose and were tucked behind her ears. Her hair even looked weary.

I began to recite the speech I had prepared: "Please don't take her from the program. Your daughter has so much promise. Please, just give us a few more years. Don't let her lose the scholarship—she cannot have it back if she quits. *Please.* How will she pay for college without it? Don't take her from me. Not yet." My nerves seemed to impede my tongue's function and my Spanish sounded suddenly so American, so stilted.

Her mother's gaze did not waver. She just sat there staring ahead, chin elevated slightly, shaking her head silently 'no.' "She can go to college next year. Right now I need her help here." My desperation began to rise, pushing the tears I held tenuously back behind my eyes forward.

I pressed harder. If she lost the scholarship, there was little chance she would return to school after taking time off. It would be too expensive, she would get into the rut of working and lose sight of her education, or she would meet a boy and end up *acompañada*—living with him, unwedded—and becoming a housewife.

At that, Jimena nodded grimly and I had to suppress my laughter at her earnestness. It seemed to strike a chord with her mother momentarily, though. Her long pause, her sideways glance at her middle daughter's child who was swaddled in the hammock napping quietly, and her distant, deliberate nod told me she understood all too well.

For a moment, I could see her youth playing out in her dark eyes: a beautiful young woman from a poor family catches the eye of a neighborhood boy. The young man starts to come around, flirting and bringing her small mementos. He promises her the world with a tenderness and electricity in his touch that makes her believe every word. The excitement of being desired, being a wife, being a mother. The possibility of something better. She had never gone to school; her family could not afford to send all the children, so only the boys went, and only through fourth grade.

The flash of betrayal that flickered across her face told me more about Jimena's father than anything else could, and suddenly her resolve returned. She looked at me again and said quietly, "I am so grateful for everything you have given my daughter, and I know you love her like she was your own daughter. I thank you for that. But she must work."

I tried a different approach: mathematical reasoning. Her scholarship brought in $75 each month. If she went out to work, she'd make an average of $5 per day. Assuming she worked five days a week, four weeks per month, she would make $100. But that's all she would ever make. El Salvador has very little upward mobility, especially for unskilled workers. Her mother pushed back: "That's still more. The scholarship doesn't cover everything."

I had anticipated we might not be able to convince her of the four-year degree. Jimena's dream was to get an English degree and I had conversed briefly with her the day before about the possibility of doing a two-year tourism degree that included an English component. I thought it might be our best bet for changing her mom's mind.

We pitched it. And at that Jimena's brother materialized at his mother's side. I later learned her brother was playing hooky from work that day. When Jimena told him I'd be coming to the house, he decided to be there to support his little sister.

"You know, she's right, *mamá*. She started this two years ago and it flew by, don't you think?" Her mother nodded. "It would just be two more just like that. Jimena deserves it more than anyone. She works so hard. Let her stay." His words were so unexpected that I fully burst into tears.

Her uncle chimed in from outside the door: "She's such a bright girl. Let her stay. I'll help with what little I can. This is a blessing for her."

And her brother continued, "Mom, listen. I promise I'll help. I'll work extra to pay for her transportation every day. You don't have to worry about that."

Desperate tears streamed down Jimena's face now, and my forehead began to throb from the frozen, pleading expression that had paralyzed my face since we began. My whole body was rigid, imploring her to reconsider, to give Jimena a chance.

The house fell silent.

After a tense moment, her mother's body went slack and she reached out and clutched my hand. Her hand was soft, conditioned by the oil she rubs in her palms to keep the tortilla masa from sticking to them. But it was strong—the hand of a person who has struggled every day of her life, hauling water, gathering firewood, wielding machetes, peeling tortillas off of hot iron *comales*. It evidenced a life more difficult than I would ever know.

Her reluctance to let Jimena study was in no way a reflection of her love for her daughter, nor were her intentions mean. It was rooted in fear and insecurity— poverty's closest friends—and reinforced by experience and culture. Our challenge was not to convince her that her daughter ought to study; it was to allay her fears about "tomorrow" and help her see beyond it to the promise of a better life with the investment, patience, and sacrifice of and for her daughter.

"*Se la dejo*. She can stay." Her face softened and her eyes closed.

I threw my arms around her slight shoulders and we sobbed together for a long instant. She pulled back and took both my hands in hers. "It's not that I don't want her to study. It's just so hard. I'm all alone. But I'm so proud of her."

Jimena has almost finished her first year of her two-year technical degree. She gets up every morning at 4:30 a.m. to sweep the leaves that have fallen on the patio during the night, prepare breakfast for her mom and siblings, leave lunch in the fridge for her mom, and then heads to school in a town an hour's bus ride away. When she returns home in the evening, she sweeps inside the house, washes laundry by hand in the cement *pila*, then begins dinner. Once all the dishes have been washed, she sits at the candlelit table with her brother to do homework and practice English until she succumbs to sleep.

Her brother has made good on his promise to help with her transportation costs, and despite the challenges Jimena faces, she is unfailingly enthusiastic about school. Her mother has not revoked her support, and in fact, seems visibly more comfortable and participatory in the monthly parent meetings. She is honored by her daughter's advancement and talks proudly about how her daughter is studying to be "a professional."

LA MAMÁS

*"Mothers in El Espino have taught me more about love
and sacrifice than anything else."*

School registration is one of the most important days
of the year for families with school-age children in rural
El Salvador. The session in which a student ends up has
huge implications for his or her safety.

Even the children who make hour-plus-long treks to
school do whatever possible to be in the morning
session because they are much less likely to have run-ins
with gang members. Nocturnal as they are, the gangs are
typically asleep when the morning session begins and
lets out, but they start their days around the time the
afternoon students get out and head home. During part
of the year, it grows dark by that hour, which further
complicates the safety situation. Mothers will do
anything to get their children into the morning session,
even when it means pushing the government-set limit of
40 students per classroom.

65

There are not only a limited number of spaces for the coveted morning session, but there are limited openings for registration, period. Teachers dread registration day because they have to turn students away while mothers plead tearfully to allow "just one more student." *Don* Paco, the beloved seventh-grade teacher who began his career at this school 40-some years ago (in fact, he helped build the school that stands today) and who had to negotiate with the government to allow him *not* to retire, regularly has 50 students in his morning session.

In November 2011, registration day fell four days after Thanksgiving in the U.S., and thus, three days after a phenomenon that has been exported to El Salvador by American and transnational companies: Black Friday. I watched as more affluent citizens lined up outside shopping malls all night long to be the first in line for the best discounts at commercial centers across the country, following a holiday *they don't even celebrate.*

Two nights later in El Espino, mothers—some from more than an hour's walk away—lined up outside the school beginning at 3:00 a.m. to be the first to register their children when the gates opened at 8:00 a.m. Monday morning. Black Friday carries a very sad irony when its significance is juxtaposed with that of the line of women in front of the school in El Espino, counting on strength in numbers and God's grace to protect them from the danger inherent in being out at that hour.

* * *

Mothers in El Espino have taught me more about love and sacrifice than anything else. Most of them grew up in times and conditions that made education beyond primary school (and in some cases any education at all) impossible. They typically became mothers at a young age and either took to maintaining the house or working extremely low-paying, laborious jobs. They have had toilsome lives, but somehow seem to never tire of giving to and for their children.

The mothers in our scholarship program are a daily source of inspiration to me. They send their children off to school every day with a blessing upon their forehead and a prayer for their safety and protection, believing in the merit of the daily sacrifice each child makes to get an education despite the prevailing danger. Some of the students leave very early and return late at night, traveling along notoriously dangerous bus routes and through communities fraught with violence. The anxiety this uncertainty undoubtedly brings a mother is overcome by her faith in both God and a better future.

These parents' genuine wish to see their children *superarse*[6] and overcome the poverty in which they live is evident in their commitment to the rules of the program, which require almost as much participation from parents as from the students. Every month, a parent or guardian must accompany each student to the scholarship meetings, which often means entrusting younger children to the care of relatives and leaving the house unattended.

The parents are, therefore, present at the compulsory monthly workshops and lectures imparted to the students, which cover topics that range from saving money to gender roles. The talks are designed to

---

[6] See footnote 2 on page 4.

broaden the students' understanding of their reality and their responsibility to their communities' development, while making them aware of cultural practices and heuristics they carry subconsciously and that influence their interactions with the world. The benefit to the parents, and especially the mothers, who participate in these workshops cannot be overstated.

Though many dedicated fathers are active in the program, the mothers are undoubtedly the backbone. They have formed a sort of extended family, one in which they have greater social capital and can turn to one another for support, and in which they are empowered to make decisions for the program that ultimately benefit their families. As a group, for example, they decided to organize monthly raffles to raise money to throw a graduation party every year for all the graduates in the program. From that they also created a small fund to have available in the event of an emergency or hardship for any one of the scholarship families.

Beginning in 2010, our delegates began to stay exclusively in the homes of scholarship students. When we arrive in the community every trip, the host mothers invariably ask me with a nervous sparkle as they eye the group of *gringos* who file anxiously out of the van at the *Casa Comunal*, the de facto community center, "Which ones are my new *hijos*? I want to introduce them to their new family."

And that is precisely what they become.

The host families care for their guests as they would their own children, with a level of attentiveness that sometimes astounds the delegates. "My mom got up in the middle of the night last night when I went out to the bathroom and waited in the doorway until I was back safely in bed." "My mom insisted on washing my feet after I played *fútbol* with the kids yesterday, then brought her sandals out for me to wear." "Our mom left the house and came back before we even woke up this morning to bring us sweet bread to have with our coffee."

Their acceptance of others is unconditional and loving. When I stopped eating meat a few years ago, the moms listened intently to my reasons for not eating meat, with no trace of judgment or disappointment (which was quite contrary to my experience with friends in the U.S.). They started planning separate vegetarian dishes for me at group meals over my protests and insistence that I was more than happy with the beans, rice, tortillas, and the myriad of sides that are customarily served with every meal.

My favorite moments with the mothers are the ones we spend together over a hot *comal*, a flat iron griddle used for making tortillas and El Salvador's national dish, *pupusas*. This is where conversations come alive, teasing is dished out heartily, and trust is fortified.

I have learned to grease my palm with warm oil before grabbing a hunk of *masa*, or corn dough, rolling it into a flattened ball, pressing a hunk of beans or cheese in the middle, folding the edges together, and rolling a new ball. I have learned how to cock my left thumb to guide the edge of the disc that is formed by gently slapping the ball between both hands and rotating it dexterously with the right. I have learned that, once on the *comal*, when the edges begin to lift and become rounded, it is time to turn the *pupusa* over, gingerly lifting from the edge with a thumb and forefinger and flipping it before it can burn you.

With the mothers of El Espino as my patient teachers, I have learned to make pupusas (*pupusear*), to wash clothes by hand, to cook over a fire, and to balance bundles on my head. I have learned ancient remedies for a myriad of maladies, to point with my lips when my hands are occupied, and that your cupped palm is the only measuring cup you need. But above all, *las mamás* have taught me how to give love like a mother—selflessly and unconditionally.

LO APRENDIDO

I find it difficult to remember life before El Salvador. I do not recognize the person I was before because El Salvador has become such an inextricable part of who I am. The approaching anniversary has made me reflect on the last decade and what it has meant to the Sister communities, the Foundation, all of those who have been touched in some way by its work, and to me personally. I think of the more than fifty travelers who have returned from El Salvador, declaring it perhaps not their most relaxing trip, but undoubtedly one of the most enriching and life-changing of their lives. I think of the friendships that have flourished both between delegates and scholarship students, and also among students and families.

For me, this decade has been one of profound personal growth, indelible experiences, and above all, invaluable lessons learned. I have been shaped by the people who have come into my life via the Foundation, by my trip-ups and mistakes, by experience, and by the

Salvadoran culture, which has embraced me as warmly as I have embraced it.

In honor of each of the last 10 years, I wish to share the 10 most profound lessons that El Salvador has taught me—*lo aprendido*.

Lesson #1: Central America is not Mexico.

In fact, Central America is a beautifully heterogeneous region with intricate, and though intertwined, distinct cultures. Over the years, I have had to gently correct a number of misguided perceptions about El Salvador. One of my favorites was on the first night of a trip to the country with a small group of delegates.

We stopped at a *pupusería* on our way from the airport to the guesthouse to dine on the country's national cuisine, the pupusa. I handed over the thin piece of paper on which I had etched our order and sat back, waiting for the waiter to arrive with beverages.

After several minutes sipping contentedly on bottled sodas and thick Salvadoran hot chocolate, 19-year-old Ali leaned over and whispered, "Where are the chips and salsa?" I smiled. "We're not in Mexico, my dear."

Ali would return to El Salvador with me three times after that trip and become a long-standing and active board member of the Foundation, but that cultural misstep was not one she lived down quickly.

In the same way, my tumbleweed-plagued dust bowl image could not have been less informed before my first trip. My first lesson, and one of which I have been constantly reminded since, was that there are so many places and cultures beyond my daily scope and that each is unique.

Lesson #2: Nothing is more important than this very moment.

My grandparents had a room in their house they called the "sitting room." But you weren't allowed to sit in it. In fact, it was completely off limits to us growing up. My grandfather died in that room and those final days with all the nurses, home help, and family members were the most traffic I had ever seen in it. It was tragically ironic; that room was being preserved for some big occasion or special visitor, but my grandpa reached the end of his life before it ever got enough use to truly justify its existence.

In El Salvador, when a guest comes to call—any guest—a host does not hesitate to bring out the nicest dishes. If the occasion is special enough, the finest rooster, turkey, or goat is slaughtered. If an unexpected guest drops by, an adult presses a few coins into the palm of one of the young children with a whispered instruction to bring soda, sweet breads, or snacks.

At first (and I mean for the first several years), I struggled with what I perceived as the culture's lackadaisical attitude towards time. I worried that a late arrival would be interpreted as disrespectful and that plans, however loosely made, were to be upheld. But with time, I learned to calm my anxiety and to settle into the present moment, dedicating all of my mental energy to the experience at hand rather than to fretting about where else I should be or what I could be doing.

For so many Salvadorans, especially in poorer rural communities like El Espino, "tomorrow" is ephemeral. The vulnerability that stems from poverty, coupled by the unpredictability of the violence, make tomorrow far from guaranteed. The company you have in this moment and the experience you are sharing is the surest thing you have, so live it. And get out the good dishes.

Lesson #3: Be creatively resourceful.

My *Papá* has been a constant example to me of creative resourcefulness. In addition to carving a new handle for his sledgehammer, I have seen him stitch a broken leg back onto a plastic patio chair, turn a curling iron package into a makeshift frame to hold an image of Jesus on the home altar, and fix countless broken items with ingenious solutions. His pickup truck is a living example of what a fix-it mentality can achieve. Despite the fact you can see the ground through rusted holes in the floor and the foam stuffing pokes out of the worn-down and depressed seats, the engine still roars when it starts.

When my new rice cooker stopped working, I searched for a small appliance repair shop in the Grand Valley that would fix it. Even with Google's assistance, I couldn't find a single shop that repairs rice cookers. When I called one appliance shop, I was told that my best bet would be to throw it away and just buy a new one.

We live in a culture in which we often throw things away too quickly and spend money heedlessly. El Salvador has taught me that most things have a lot more life in them than we give them credit for and that persistence, creativity, and resourcefulness can extend the usefulness of things we simply discard.

Lesson #4: If you wake up in the morning with breath in your lungs, you get up and work hard for something better.

A hardworking, persistent spirit is a trademark of all the families I have stayed with in El Espino. From the students who awaken before dawn to get ready for school and stay up long past dark studying to the adults who fill almost every waking hour with productive activity, I am in a state of perpetual admiration.

I've encountered women of all ages who wake up at daybreak and somehow finish the *aseo*—the house cleaning—which generally includes sweeping and mopping inside, raking or sweeping aside fallen leaves outside, and often doing the household's wash by hand, all before breakfast. I've watched with awe as children perform chores dutifully and without protest, and as men labor at jobs in sweltering, humid heat from sunup to sundown. And when the workday is over, they gather to work on digging trenches or mixing concrete to extend paved roads deeper into the community.

My *Papá* and *Mamá*, both now in their eighties, work harder than people I know who are half their age. One late morning I sat with my *Mamá* at the kitchen table as I finished my coffee. She had just finished washing the breakfast dishes and feeding all the animals. I asked her where my *Papá* was. He had slipped away right after breakfast. She responded that he was already out working in the land behind the house, and as I shook my head in amazement, she smiled. "If I don't let him work, he'll die," she said simply. And I think she might be right.

I admit that I have days that I wake up and simply don't feel like doing much. Self-employment exacerbates the situation because some days I don't have to be in any place at any particular time. But after living with families in El Espino and watching their drive, those days have become rarer for me and are always accompanied without a tremendous feeling of guilt. No amount of *hueva*, or feelings of laziness, is enough to keep my *Papá* from being in constant motion, and that is enough to remind me to keep me moving.

Lesson #5: Things die. People die. Sometimes horribly. But you have to keep living.

The national Salvadoran newspapers I read every day are smattered with stories of death. Kenia's story, though heartbreaking, is not unique; every Salvadoran can tell of someone close to them who has died or been killed. During a visit one year, a man was mistakenly targeted by gang members just up the road from my *Papá's* house in broad daylight as he returned home from work with his wife and small niece. When I passed the spot the next day, the talc powder on the road masked the blood, but stood as a chilling reminder of the fragility of life.

Sadly, Salvadoran children understand death in a way that I couldn't grasp until I was well into my adult years, and perhaps I still cannot. But they also understand that life doesn't come to a halt for those left behind. Perhaps this is a result of the deep-rooted influence of the Catholic faith and its teachings on eternal life, or perhaps it is just the Salvadoran survival instinct. In any case, El Salvador has taught me how to mourn the death of loved ones while still honoring the life that courses through my veins. Kenia's vitality is testament to that.

Lesson # 6: Family matters.

I come from an extended family that is scattered across the United States. We used to see each other at infrequent family reunions and now are connected very impersonally through social media. Even my nuclear family, despite living in the same town, doesn't get together very regularly. There is an unspoken understanding that each of us is busy and has their own life that runs somewhere parallel to, but not intertwined with, the life of the family. Family unity was never a core value for us, which is not to say that we do not love each other deeply. We just do it from a distance.

When I was welcomed into the homes of families in El Salvador, I was humbled by the loyalty and sacrifice that exists within the family unit. Brothers and sisters, and even cousins and neighbors, share without bitterness and offer each other genuine support. Extended family is as much a part of daily life as the nuclear family and it is not uncommon for many generations to live under one roof, mutually contributing to the maintenance of the household and the upbringing of children. In times of danger and hardship, such as the tropical depression I witnessed in 2011, family takes on an even greater role, as one's very survival may depend on it.

As the families in the community have unconditionally welcomed me into their lives, I have experienced this loving and generous kind of family unity firsthand. I have gained perspective with regard to my own family, humility when it comes to inviting others into my life as El Salvador has welcomed me, and a broader understanding of what unites a family.

Lesson # 7: Give generously.

I never saw the young woman who gave me her shirt after that day. I never even learned her name. Her action was entirely selfless, an anonymous gesture from which she stood nothing to gain. And she is but one of many stories of generosity that I have experienced in El Salvador.

One year, I forgot to make arrangements for a ride from the airport or a reservation at the guest house. I found myself stranded at the Salvadoran airport at night with nowhere to go, and a woman who had been sitting a few seats away from me on the airplane insisted that I not only come home with her that night, but that I also stay for Thanksgiving dinner with her entire family the next night.

On more than one occasion, families have graciously offered to host our delegates, even when it meant that the whole family would have to sleep together in one bed or in hammocks in order to make a bed available to their guests. And the sacrifice does not stop there—they go to great lengths to ensure the comfort of the delegates, never expecting anything in return.

The last day in El Espino on my first trip, I stood with a cluster of children from the ages of two to 15 behind my host home as everyone else boarded the bus for the capital. These kids had been my companions throughout my two-week homestay and saying goodbye to them was one of the most brutal emotions I had ever felt.

One of the older boys who had seemed the most reluctant to get close to me during the trip waited until very last to approach me. As he embraced me, I felt him press something into my palm as he whispered tearfully,

"*Te quiero, hermana.*" I love you, sister.

I didn't open my palm until I was on the bus and what I saw was a large gold crucifix pendant lined with what looked like diamonds. I would later find out he won it in a swimming contest with another boy and that it was his most expensive possession. I wore that cross under my clothing for years as a reminder of the fire that was lit in my heart on that first trip.

My home is filled with tiny mementos of love I have received over the years, given to me by people and children who, by world standards, live well below the poverty line; people whose generosity is not constrained by their financial resources, but instead is offered unreservedly. These are my treasures and serve as daily reminders that we should always strive to give of ourselves in whatever ways we can.

Lesson #8: Paternalistic charity does no long-term good in the developing world.

Though emergency relief efforts have their place in the world of international aid, unless systemic problems are addressed, we will always be applying billion dollar Band-Aids to situations that are the consequence of those problems. Economic inequality, ineffective or corrupt governance, access to and distribution of resources, barriers to education (cultural, geographic, ideological, or otherwise), and lack of conscientization and empowerment are among the myriad of deep-seeded societal ills that plague El Salvador and most of the developing and underdeveloped world. The focus of international aid should be on finding solutions to these issues.

Our assistance following Hurricane Ida met an immediate need and undoubtedly meant the world to the three families who received funding to rebuild their homes. But in the big picture, the families still live in the vulnerability in which they lived before the storm hit, even after constructing new homes. The new houses were sturdier, but a sturdy home did not keep them from having to make difficult decisions in the interest of their livelihood and survival, ultimately giving up the homes they received in two of the three cases. Instead, our efforts to provide educational and vocational opportunities to students and residents in El Espino will have much more lasting effects and will ultimately better equip the community to respond to crises like natural disasters.

Larger development efforts may require more patience and have less immediate feel-good results than projects like service trips in which Americans travel to places in need to build or buy things, but they do more long-term good. These efforts must empower people to identify and craft solutions to their problems, enlist them as active partners in promoting change, and create a sense of ownership in their own development projects. There is no room for paternalism in today's paradigm of development work; instead solidarity and the humanization of those receiving assistance to those providing it should be guiding principles.

As we learned after Hurricane Ida, we can build as many houses as we want, but until we help provide opportunities that give people resources and allow them to be the architects of their own development, our efforts are fruitless.

Lesson # 9: *Education is the best bet for overcoming poverty.*

Poverty creates cyclical traps, particularly in the developing world, that are incredibly difficult to overcome, one of which is the dismal future for young people who are unable to get an education. The lack of resources in these countries creates an imperative need for young people to abandon their education and go to work to help support themselves and their family, which then limits their opportunities to obtain better-paying employment. Both empirical studies and anecdotal evidence point to education as a deterrent to early pregnancy, so young people who are unable to continue going to school often have children at a young age, children who then fall victim to the same trap that their parents fell in. What results is generational poverty that is nearly impossible to escape.

Jimena's mom was a victim of this kind of generational poverty, as are so many of the residents of El Espino and El Salvador as a whole. Her mother's mentality was not culpable, but rather one that had been inculcated in her from an early age and that was born of necessity. Jimena was at risk of following the same path that her mother and so many before her had traveled, were it not for the opportunity she earned to continue her studies through a scholarship.

An education does not just provide academic and professional skills, but it also broadens a student's manner of thinking and his or her worldviews. Education is not a be-all and end-all; it is an opportunity—an opportunity to change paradigms at the individual level, which then transfers to the family and community. This kind of conscientization is crucial to encouraging students to identify the societal patterns that prevent development and progress, especially the patterns of poverty itself, and to propose solutions. In El Salvador, education also can play an even more critical role, as it serves as a prosocial deterrent to the allure of gangs and other illicit groups.

Many of our scholarship students are first-generation high school graduates and come from families with one or more illiterate parents. Most of them are also the first in their family to attend college. But the values that they are now learning in school and through the scholarship program are passed on to their siblings and the example these students set will ripple beyond their immediate families and into their communities.

This generation of students in El Espino will have more opportunities than their parents' generation to earn a living wage and as they graduate and return to their communities to practice their respective fields, the communities will also benefit from having professional doctors, lawyers, nurses, teachers, translators, accountants, and more who are committed to serving the community and contributing to its development. These students will eventually have children, as well, who will be raised with an emphasis on education, effectively breaking the cycle of poverty.

As aid dollars around the world are allocated to the diverse problems afflicting poverty-stricken regions, access to education must be a top priority. The FCE scholarship program is the cornerstone of its work in El Espino.

Lesson #10: Give your love before it is earned.

Opening the doors of one's home to complete strangers from distant lands requires a level of trust that is beyond most people's comprehension. Bestowing upon them titles of *hermano/hermana*, *hijo/hija*, or simply *familia* from the moment they enter the home is a deeper offering of love than many are even capable of. Yet this is exactly what happens in El Espino.

One of our delegates remarked to me after her first couple of days in the community that she couldn't believe how loved she felt. "They didn't wait to know who I was. They simply gave me their love when I walked in that door." Many of our travelers have expressed similar sentiments, and the last day in the community is always tearful on the part of both host and guest.

Ten years in El Salvador have given me more love than I could earn in a lifetime. But they have also taught me my own capacity to love—without reservation, without condition, and without fear.

EPILOGUE

El Espino has become a home to me as much physically as emotionally. When I pull up to my *Papá*'s house, it feels much like pulling up to my childhood home and finding everything and everyone intact and just as I left it. There is *Mamá*, leaning in the doorway to the kitchen in her purple flowered apron, her silver hair braided smartly at the nape of her neck and her hands glistening with cooking oil. Smoke billows from the fire lit under the *comal* where she has been busy *torteando*. *Papá* ambles up in his white t-shirt and weathered ball cap, machete in hand, and offers a warm, fraternal side-hug.

I step inside the cinderblock home and am ushered in by familiar sights: the grayish-red tiled floor spreading beneath drab floral furniture that must have been regal in its day; the lazy hammock hanging limply across the living room; the makeshift shrine behind the dining room table adorned with its blue-and-white checkered tablecloth; the TV blaring a pompous cacophony of *reguetón* music, news, and celebrity gossip; the old school desk in the middle of the room piled high with papers and mementos from *Mamá*'s trip to Australia; and at the far end of the room, the dingy floral curtain shrouding the entryway to the bedroom I share with my *hermanitas*. More than anything, the faces that greet me remind me that I am home.

ABOUT THE FOUNDATION FOR CULTURAL EXCHANGE

The Foundation for Cultural Exchange was founded in 2004 by a group of travelers who wanted to nurture the spark that was lit inside each one of us on that first trip and keep it burning. We got together and incorporated the organization, then petitioned the Grand Junction City Council to adopt the small community of El Espino as its Sister City, which finally received a unanimous vote in September 2005. In the meantime, the FCE worked with Immaculate Heart of Mary Catholic Parish, which was in the process of selecting a church as a sister parish, to formalize a relationship with the local parish in El Espino and planned its first return delegation to the country for the following summer.

The mission of the FCE is to promote cultural understanding and solidarity between the people of Western Colorado and El Espino, El Salvador through cultural immersion trips, economic and social development, promoting education, and formal Sister organization relationships. The organization has five pillars: the David C. Harmon Memorial Scholarship program, community development projects in El Espino, Sister relationships (currently a Sister Parish, three Sister Schools, and a Sister Library), cultural immersion trips, and awareness efforts in the Grand Valley.

The FCE works hand-in-hand with El Espino in a way that preserves and promotes the dignity of its residents while empowering them to identify and resolve their own problems. This makes them architects of their own development, which increases the likelihood that the changes that take place will have lasting impact. The greatest problems in El Salvador stem from a lack of opportunities—above all economic and educational—so the FCE aims to foster an environment in which such opportunities are within reach for more of its people.

The FCE carries out its work in collaboration with the Centro de Intercambio y Solidaridad (CIS) in San Salvador to administer the scholarship program and carry out community projects. The relationship has been described by the CIS as a three-legged stool; the community, the FCE, and the CIS exist co-dependently and if one leg were absent, the stool would collapse. For more information about CIS and its work throughout El Salvador, visit www.cis-elsalvador.org.

The scholarship program is the cornerstone of the FCE because it both educates El Espino's young people academically and inculcates a sense of ownership and responsibility in the community's youth, which we believe will have immeasurable ripple effects as they become professionals who serve their own community, and later parents who will instill the same values in their children. Instead of the exodus of young people to the United States we are currently experiencing, we hope to eventually see a country where young people can stay and thrive, but this can only happen if more opportunities are made available to the country's youth.

What makes the FCE scholarship program unique is the fact that we guarantee our students' scholarships from the first year of high school through their college graduation. Sixteen-year-olds enter high school with the broad vision earning college diploma, not just finishing high school. What's more, each student is paired with sponsors in the U.S. with whom they correspond throughout the year. This creates a sense of accountability and the feeling that somebody is pulling for them, which is an impressive source of motivation for the students.

To date, 17 students have graduated high school on FCE scholarships, 16 are currently enrolled in college, and eight more are enrolled in high school. Each year, the program adds four new first-year high school students selected by a committee made up of current scholarship parents, teachers at the local school, and community members. (The FCE does not participate in the selection process.) Sponsorships are $300/year for high school students and $1,000/year for university students. To become a sponsor or learn more about our current students, visit our webpage at www.FCEelsalvador.org.

ABOUT THE AUTHOR

ANNA M. STOUT is a founding member of the
Foundation for Cultural Exchange and has served as its
president since 2004. She has returned to the country more
than 35 times since her first visit. Ms. Stout is also a
Certified Translator (Spanish>English) by the American
Translators Association, a Certified Court Interpreter by
the State of Colorado, and a Forensic Transcription and
Translation Specialist. She owns Transfinem Language and
Cultural Services, a regional translation, interpretation, and
cultural consulting company (www.transfinem.com). Ms.
Stout travels frequently around the western United States
giving cultural trainings and serves on numerous nonprofit boards in the Grand Valley. She divides her time
between Grand Junction, CO, El Espino, El Salvador, and
exploring the rest of the world. She is a self-proclaimed
word nerd and chronic sojourner.

16385751R00065

Made in the USA
San Bernardino, CA
01 November 2014